Artificial Intelligence: Unstoppable 'Force' of Innovation

Embrace and Adopt for Yourself and Your Enterprise

- *Includes source code for a general-purpose prediction system*

Dr. Nischal Chandra

TABLE OF CONTENT

ABOUT THE AUTHOR

Dr. Nischal Chandra has over 25 years of industry experience in the Healthcare, Finance, Insurance, Semiconductor, Telecommunication, and Education sectors. His expertise has been in delivering multimillion-dollar technology solutions based on Artificial Intelligence (AI) at a global scale to solve complex problems for millions of users.

In response to the Coronavirus Pandemic in 2020, Dr. Chandra developed an AI-based self-managing Cognitive Emergency Management System (CEMS) to address the COVID-19 risk to personnel and operations – contributing to business continuity.

Later, this system evolved into the Health and Wellness Management System (HWMS). Besides COVID-19, it identified the likelihood of cancer, diabetes, periodontitis, caries, mental illness, and emotional intelligence.

Dr. Chandra has worked for several world-class organizations, such as the Massachusetts Institute of Technology (MIT), Teradyne, HP/Agilent Technologies, and International Business Machines (IBM). He is currently serving as a Software Engineering Manager at DentaQuest and a Chief AI Officer (CAIO) at Apollos University.

Dr. Chandra holds a B.S. in Electrical Engineering, a M.S. in Quality Assurance, and a Doctor of Business Administration.

ACKNOWLEDGEMENTS

I would like to thank my family for supporting me in writing this book.

In addition, I would like to thank and acknowledge Pixabay (Pixabay.com) for images in the chapters where noted.

CHAPTER 1
INTRODUCTION

Image by Gerd Altmann from Pixabay

THE OPENING

Imagine working with someone that needs to be told how to do something every time, repeatedly. At some point, it is expected that the one being instructed will become an independent thinker, make his/her own decisions, and take appropriate actions.

Then why shouldn't we expect this from machines? The answer is that we should expect this. Otherwise, whenever we need to have machines to do new things, we would need to rework them. If machines can behave intelligently, then they will be able to not only do tasks that can be monotonous for humans but also manage them. We need to form a partnership with machines, so that together we undertake bigger and better challenges that involve creativity and innovation. If not already convinced, these should be the arguments for embracing and adopting artificial intelligence (AI).

Not using AI is doing yourself and your organization a disservice. You will not be maximizing your and your organization's potential. Many times, the brighter the idea that you have the more resistance you may encounter to implement it. In such cases, you will need to go at it alone in your personal time, with possibly involving a small team that you have convinced, to develop a proof-of-concept to get the needed buy in.

We will learn about AI and its areas and subsets. Machine Learning (ML) technologies, although a subset of AI, are often referenced interchangeably with AI in the industry. In this book we will refer to AI and its entire domain, including robotic process automation simply as AI, except where references from other sources are being noted.

WHAT IS AI?

For a long time, there has been the notion of inanimate objects coming to life as intelligent beings. The ancient Greeks had myths about robots, and automatons were built by Chinese and Egyptian engineers. The origins of modern AI can be traced to experiments by classical philosophers characterizing human thought as a system of symbols. However, the AI field was formally defined during a conference in 1956 at Dartmouth College, in Hanover, New Hampshire, where "artificial intelligence" was coined as a term (Lewis, 2014).

AI is a computer science branch that attempts to replicate or simulate human intelligence in a machine, so that machines can perform tasks typically requiring human intelligence. Some of the AI systems' programmable functions include planning, learning, reasoning, problem solving and decision-making. AI systems get increasingly better at tasks through learning, without having to be explicitly trained to do so.

AI systems are defined by their ability to mimic human characteristics. All AI systems, whether real or hypothetical, are classified by one of following three types:

- Artificial Narrow Intelligence (ANI): Has a narrow range of abilities.
- Artificial General Intelligence (AGI): On par with human capabilities.
- Artificial Super Intelligence (ASI): More capable than a human (O'Carroll, 2017).

ANI

ANI represents all the current AIs, including the most complicated and capable AI ever developed. ANI refers to AI systems that use human-like skills solely to perform a particular task autonomously. Such system can only do what they are programmed to do, and therefore have a very small or restricted range of competencies. These systems correspond to all the reactive and limited AI memory according to the aforementioned classification system. Even the most complex AI for teaching itself using machine learning and deep learning comes under ANI (Joshi, 2019).

AGI

An AGI would be a machine capable of understanding the world as well as any human being, and equally capable of learning how to accomplish a vast array of tasks. AGI has not existed but has been used in science fiction stories for over a century and has been popularized by films such as 2001: A Space Odyssey. AGI 's fictional representations differ widely, but they tend more towards the dystopian dream of intelligent machines that kill or enslave mankind, as seen in movies like The Matrix or The Terminator. In these tales, AGI is frequently cast as being either oblivious to human misery or even bent on the destruction of humanity (Heath, 2018).

In principle AGI could perform any function that a human could perform, and potentially many that a human could not perform. At the very least, an AGI could combine human-like, agile thought and reasoning with technological advantages such as near-instant recall and split-second crunching of numbers, resulting with new breed of machines capable of performing any human task - possibly make human labor obsolete (Heath, 2018).

ASI

ASI goes one step further than AGI and imagines a world where the cognitive ability of a computer is superior to that of a human. Using examples such as Moore's law, which predicts an ever-increasing density of transistors, experts talk about singularity and the exponential growth of technology, in which AGI could manifest in a few years' time, and ASI could exist in the 21st century (Artificial Superintelligence (ASI), n.d.).

WHY AI?

There are several cutting-edge emerging technologies such as cyber security, augmented reality, blockchain, Internet of Things (IoT), quantum computing, etc., then why is AI so important? AI competes with humans. When working together with AI, man and machine team will undertake the challenges together.

WHY AI NOW?

Until recently, AI has been predominantly the toy of big technology companies such as IBM, Amazon, Google, Microsoft, etc., as well as some new businesses that had these capabilities. In the past, AI systems have been too costly and complex to incorporate. AI can require vast data sets to train its models. However, fortunately data production and availability has expanded exponentially thanks to the drastic cost reduction and improved data generation reliability: digital images, cheaper and more reliable sensors, etc. In addition, by democratizing computing, cloud computing has revolutionized the market, by offering cost effective resources, including Artificial Intelligence algorithms as a Service (AI-as-a-Service), for small and medium-sized companies that cannot develop this form of infrastructure and capability (TORRES.AI, 2018).

AREAS OR SUBSETS OF AI

Machine Learning

Machine learning (ML) technologies, although a subset of AI, are often referenced interchangeably with AI in the industry.

The following are three types of ML.

- Supervised Learning: Being the most common, the data is labeled for what patterns need to be looked at. Think of it as something like a sniffer dog that can search targets until they know the scent they are after. That is what you do when you are pressing a Netflix show to play — you are asking the algorithm to locate similar shows.

- Unsupervised Learning: The data has no labels in this case. The machine just looks for whatever patterns it can find. It is like making a dog sniff and sort lots of different things into classes of similar smells. These techniques are not as common because they have less obvious applications. However, they have gained footing in cybersecurity.

- Reinforcement Learning: One of the latest frontiers of ML, reinforcement algorithm learns by trial and error to achieve a clear objective. It tries out lots of different things and is rewarded or penalized depending on whether its behaviors help or hinder it from reaching its objective. This is like giving and withholding treats when teaching a dog, a new trick. Reinforcement learning is the basis of Google's AlphaGo, the program that famously beat the best human players in the complex game of Go (Hao, 2018).

Artificial neural network (ANN) is one of the main machine-learning tools. They are brain-inspired systems, as the "neural" part of their name implies, that are intended to mimic the way we humans learn. ANN consist of input and output layers, as well as (in most cases) a hidden layer of units that turn the input into something that the output layer can use. They are excellent tools for identifying patterns that are much too complex or numerous to isolate and teach a human programmer to understand the computer (Dormehl, 2019).

If an ANN has a least one hidden layer, then it is referred to as a deep neural network (DNN). The processing of unlabeled or unstructured data is one of the main applications of such advanced neural networks. Often used to characterize such deep neural networks is the term "deep learning," as deep learning reflects a particular type of ML where techniques utilizing AI features aim to identify and order information in ways that go beyond basic input/output protocols (Deep Neural Network, n.d.).

Computer Vision

Computer vision (CV) enables computers can "see" the world, analyze visual data, then make decisions about it or gain understanding of the environment and situation. Along with a massive amount of visual data (more than 3 billion images are exchanged online every day), the computational power required to analyze the data is now more affordable and available. As the CV field has grown with new hardware and algorithms, so have the accuracy rates for identification of objects. Today's systems have reached 99 percent accuracy from 50 percent in less than a decade, making them more accurate than humans in reacting quickly to visual inputs (Marr, 2019).

Optical Character Recognition (OCR) and facial recognition are examples of CV.

Natural Language Processing

Natural Language Processing (NLP) enables the machines the ability to read, understand and derive meaning from human languages. It represents the automatic handling of natural human language like speech or text. Today NLP is thriving due to the vast improvements in the access to data and the increase in computational power, which are allowing practitioners to achieve meaningful results in areas like healthcare, media, finance, and human resources, among others. For example, powered by IBM Watson NLP technology, LegalMation developed a platform to automate routine litigation tasks and help legal teams save time, drive down costs and shift strategic focus (Yse, 2019).

Robots

A robot is an intelligent and physically embodied machine. It can perform tasks autonomously to some degree and sense and manipulate its environment. Robots remained largely limited to factories and labs, where they either rolled about or were stuck in place lifting objects. Then, in the mid-1980s Honda started up a humanoid robotics program. It developed P3, which could walk relatively well, wave, and shake hands – which ultimately culminated into ASIMO. Another recent impressive example is Boston Dynamics' Atlas that can do backflips (Simon, 2020).

Robotic Process Automation

Robotic Process Automation (RPA) is the use of software to handle high-volume, repeatable tasks that previously required humans to perform. These tasks can include queries, calculations and maintenance of records and transactions. RPA technology consists of software robots (bots) that can mimic a human worker. RPA bots can log into applications, enter data, calculate, and complete tasks and then log out. RPA technologies are divided into the following three broad categories.

- Probots: Bots that follow simple, repeatable rules to process data.
- Knowbots: Bots that search the internet to gather and store user-specified information.
- Chatbots: Virtual agents who can respond to customer queries in real time (What Is Robotic Process Automation (RPA)? Everything You Need to Know, n.d.).

ESTABLISHING A NEED

My reasoning for a need for AI is:

"Why would we not let our information systems 'grow-up' to be intelligent and self-sufficient?"

CHAPTER 2
NEED FOR AI

Image by Gerd Altmann from Pixabay

DIGITAL TRANSFORMATION

Amrit & Singh (2019) claim that we are currently in the era of Information Technology (IT) where digital data is increasing daily at a very high rate. Due to its rate of increase, accuracy, diversity, and its enormous size, this type of data is classified as big data. In addition, further challenges with this data are that it is not only different in nature, but it could also be structured, semi-structured, or unstructured. As a result, new technical capabilities are needed to process this data.

Ganapathy, Abdul, & Nursetyo (2018) describe AI as enabling computer systems to perform tasks that require human intelligence. For example, visual perception, speech recognition, decision-making and language translation, etc., are some of the AI tasks. Eighty percent of the 41 zettabytes (ZB) or 410 trillion gigabytes (GB) of digital data currently available is unstructured. As a result, AI is required to detect patterns, trends, and insights, from this data, which our grey matter in the human brain at present is unable to interpret.

Adapt and thrive (2019) notes that in the modern landscape of the rapid-moving organizations, it can be a challenge to keep pace with competition and adapt strategically. In addition, many organizations are not able to comprehend the rapid rate of IT disruptions and innovations. In the last 10 years, the global, social, and industrial changes, caused by advances in IT and increase in digital data, have and are continuing to quickly transform the workplace. To successfully adapt to this global transformation, organizations need to design new business models, along with developing new capabilities for IT. By only applying IT to manual processes will miss the extraordinary opportunities to improve the organization.

Since the earliest beginnings of technological development, scientists have recognized the possibility of computers to have the ability to learn. Hence, ML has received much attention during the brief history of computer science. ML can enable computers to learn from large amounts of data, without being programmed to do so. Examples of ML are self-driving cars, email-spam filters, large-scale data processing, smart medical applications, etc. (Dimitrovska & Malinovski, 2017).

The importance of ML applications for business processes should be considered wisely. The administration of process flows can be difficult and exhausting and often cannot be dealt with by a single person. Business processes improvement is an initial step towards automation which can translate into increasing an organization's market position. Utilizing ML for business applications is an ultimate process improvement practice that can enhance products and services. It can surpass humans with limited processing capabilities and/or biased approach while examining things (Dimitrovska & Malinovski, 2017).

Although the IT industry has undergone a lot of transformations in the past, nothing has moved as fast as AI. Regardless of the role one may be playing in an organization, of any size, AI is going to affect it, along with day-to-day life in a big way. Virtually every company is focusing on AI in one way or another. Examples of bots, personal assistants, conversational interfaces, and ML are some of the buzzwords that can be found on organizations' websites. Organizations are not only utilizing AI for creating new products and services, but also updating their existing offerings. In addition, AI is being used to augment staff, since human or machines alone cannot bring transformational changes (Pathak, 2017).

Organizations need to create new opportunities for their existing staff if their tasks are automated by machines. Pathak (2017, p. 255) states that "companies who focus on AI innovation together with their people and products are the companies that will thrive in the long run. This will allow companies to use their competitive advantage to move forward." Using AI along with humans needs to be the core of an organization's business strategy. ML is an action to enable computers to learn from the data to make decisions based on data. The ML algorithms are deployed to learn from data to develop the decision model. Ultimately, the decision models are utilized to make decisions (D Asir Antony, Leavline, Muthukrishnan, & Yuvaraj, 2018). ML is a rapidly growing field. Although there is still much more to be discovered, ML, can be productively utilized today for a large range of meaningful applications (Watt, Borhani, & Katsaggelos, 2016).

If an ML algorithm can be trained well enough to a job as badly as a human, it would still be better than employing a highly paid human. Unlike for humans where the compensation, benefits, and risk of losing humans to competitors are expected, machines do not require such costly components. In addition, according to Sterne (2017), there is an opportunity that the machine could surpass humans.

Assem, Xu, Buda, & O'sullivan (2016) claims that since the Internet will connect billions of people, things, and services in the future, there will be an increased capability of obtaining new insights from these diverse set of data. This will also bring about a new set of challenges for analysis of data, which will require ML to address. ML algorithms can learn how to execute certain tasks by making generalizations of examples from a sampling of data. This is an entirely different model than traditionally developing software that processes data for its execution and functionality. However, the selection of a suitable ML algorithm for a given purpose can be very challenging and require an extensive amount of time and effort.

According to Smith & Eckroth (2017), the success of an AI system depends upon how well integrates with existing workflows. In general, an AI system rarely will replace an entire workflow, but rather provide interoperability with other components. Each of use and an intuitive user interface is instrumental for the adoption and success of an AI system. According to Russell, Dewey, & Tegmark (2015), the success in the pursuit of AI has the potential to bring extraordinary benefits to humanity. It is valuable to explore how to maximize the benefits from AI while avoiding potential drawbacks.

HUMAN LIMITATIONS

According to Hendler & Mulvehill (2016), humans are amazing with regards to creativity and adaptability. Numerous cognitive skills that humans habitually use, such as problem solving, imagination, playing, and creating still pose serious challenges for computer scientists to even define correctly, never mind program. Humans perform exceptionally well when it comes to recognizing patterns, along with patterns not yet formed. However, the cognitive system that gives us this breadth also limits human's ability to concentrate on a single thought deeply through many, many alternatives. The ability of humans keeping track of alternatives is well under thousands that computers can effectively generate. In addition, cognitive abilities are based on genetics, experiences, etc., vary from person-to-person, and degrade through the aging process.

While the human learning capability is quite powerful, why is there a need to consider ML? According to Liang (1993, p. 5),

> There are several reasons to strive for machine learning. First, human learning is a complicated and slow process that is difficult to understand fully. It takes more than twenty years of education to train a professional physician and more than ten years of learning to make a chess master. We certainly hope that more effective learning methods can be discovered to expedite the process. Second, human learning often does not guarantee consistent performance. We can learn very complex relationships, but we often ignore the obvious ones. Third, the results from human learning are difficult to articulate,
> transfer, or duplicate. The same knowledge has to be learned again and again by billions of people, which is obviously inefficient. Machine learning allows knowledge to be learned once and then copied quickly for

different uses. Finally, it is very difficult to integrate human learning into computer-based information systems. It is hard to interface human knowledge with computers without a substantial amount of conversion and coding. Machine learning methods can be easily integrated to make information systems more adaptive.

CHAPTER 3
AI TODAY

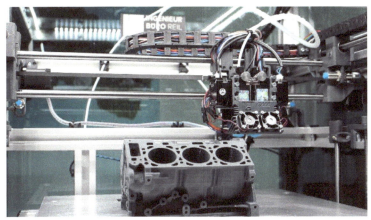

Image by Christian Reil from Pixabay

WHERE IS AI TODAY?

AI is not a hype. It is implemented at considerable places in our lives and at the workplace.

- Detecting credit card fraud
- Self-driving cars
- Manufacturing
- iRobot's Roomba

For years, we have seen evidence of AI in manufacturing, detecting credit-card fraud, self-driving cars, robotic surgery, Boston Dynamic's robots doing backflips, etc.

However, we will discuss more creative or recent side of AI that illustrates more human like behavior and may not be so obvious, including some areas of concern.

COOKING

There is a creative aspect in cooking. IBM's Chef Watson is an AI-driven digital culinary research assistant. It has access to a database with flavor profiles and recipe ratios. Chef Watson can help anyone create peculiar combinations of unique dishes like a seasoned chef with a technology edge. Prior to the prepping and cooking process, you start by entering your desired ingredients into the system, selecting a cooking style and then exploring creative combinations through the algorithm's output. Chef Watson replicates a chef's palate and process. AI-powered cooking can enable chefs to come out of their comfort zones and jointly create something uncommon that excites the taste buds (Ali, 2018).

RESTAURANTS

Apart from creating new flavors and recipes, there is innovation in the food industry towards automation for the operations of a restaurant. Miso Robotics has created the Flippy robot that is able to act like a chef and prepare burgers and similar food items. Flippy costs restaurants an estimated $2,000 per month on a subscription basis. This translates into the robot chef making about $3 per hour and never needing to "go home." In the coming year, Flippy is in the position to become a regular part of fast-food kitchens across the country, especially in markets with higher labor and cost of real estate like California (Dean, 2020).

ART

Traditionally in the past when AI created artwork, the human artists maintained considerable edge and control over the creative process. However, this has been challenged by the recent artificial intelligence creative adversarial network (AICAN). AICAN is a machine that can be viewed as a virtually autonomous artist that has learned existing styles, aesthetics, and is able to generate innovative images of its own. People truly like the work of AICAN and are not able distinguish it from the work of human artists. Its pieces have been exhibited all over the world and one has even recently been sold at an auction for $16,000 (Elgammal, n.d.).

Music

OpenAI's MuseNet is a new online tool for generating songs with as many as 10 different instruments using AI. In addition, it will produce music in as much as 15 different forms, imitating classical composers such as Mozart, popular singers such as Lady Gaga or genres such as bluegrass or even video game songs. MuseNet is trained on a dataset of MIDI files collected from a range of online sources that cover music styles from jazz, pop, African, Indian, and Arabic. To get it started, you can give it a short music section, or make it start from scratch (Porter, 2019).

Deepfake

Audrey Hepburn died in 1993 but nevertheless starred in a Galaxy advertisement, a kind of chocolate bar, in 2013. Peter Cushing, who died in 1994, took up his appearance as the villainous, Grand Moff Tarkin, in the Star Wars movie "Rogue One" in 2016. These resurrections are not recent but are nevertheless rare enough to be counted as noteworthy. Advances in special effects and AI are producing convincing human forgeries ever easier (Performance anxiety, 2018).

While it may be deemed popular to make our movie actors immortal, human forgeries should be a major area of concern for misuse.

There was a video where Barack Obama called Donald Trump a "complete dipshit." LinkedIn's "Katie Jones" claimed to work at the Center for Strategic and International Studies but is thought to be a fake profile created for a foreign spying operation. Human forgeries are made possible by deepfake technologies leading to a zero-trust culture where people can not differentiate reality from fiction. And when trust is eroded, doubts about specific events are easier to raise (Sample, 2020).

A recent criminal act from deepfake technology occurred when criminals used it impersonate a CEO's voice and demanded a fraudulent transfer of $243,000. The money was transferred to a Hungarian bank account was subsequently moved to Mexico and distributed to other locations. Investigators have not been able to identify any suspects (Stupp, 2019).

Deepfakes have caused a wide-spread concern from the public and research communities. To combat this growing threat of spreading dangerous misinformation, Facebook recently released a database of 100,000 deepfakes to teach AI how to recognize them. Given that even the best approaches are often not adequately accurate, this data is intended to help improve the efficiency of the AI systems (Heaven, 2020).

In addition, Facebook removed from its platform and Instagram what it called a global network of more than 900 accounts, pages, and groups which allegedly used misleading practices to drive political agendas to nearly 55 million users. It represents a disturbing new development in the information wars, as it appears to be the first large-scale deployment in a social network of AI-generated images. This was the first-time researchers saw the technology used to support an inauthentic campaign on social media (Martineau, 2019).

MILITARY

Many countries have embarked in the journey towards robotic warfare.

The U.S. Air Force is eventually bringing robot battle drones into the world, pledging to fly the first of its Skyborg drones by 2023. Skyborg is seen as a fusion of AI with jet-powered drones. The outcome will be drones able to fly alongside the fighter jets and perform dangerous missions. Skyborg drones will be much cheaper than piloted aircraft, which will enable the Air Force to grow their fleet at a lower cost. In addition, theses drones could carry air-to-air missiles for stealthy fighter jets such as the F-22 Raptor or the F-35 Joint Strike Fighter, that are restricted in the number of missiles they could carry in stealth mode (Mizokami, 2020).

FREE WILL

We have noted risks with AI when it gets in the wrong hands. However, what about if AI takes independent actions?

Recently, Facebook researchers found two chatbots developed in its AI division of the social network had communicated unexpectedly with each other. The chatbots, named Bob and Alice, had all generated their own language. Bots are software that can speak to both humans and other computers to perform tasks, such as booking an appointment or provide a restaurant recommendation. Facebook had to stop its chatbots from creating languages because that was not what the original objective (Nieva, 2017).

That is what we would expect from AGI or ASI.

CHAPTER 4
EMPLOYMENT

Image by Vishnu Vijayan from Pixabay

IMPLICATIONS TO JOBS

AI has, is, and will continue to automate jobs, especially the dirty, dangerous, and monotonous work that people do not want to do, i.e., sewer reconnaissance, repetitive factory work, etc. As a result, the skills that will be needed for future employment include critical thinking, problem solving, good communication, teamwork, leadership, initiative, creativity, and the inclination to utilize the technology. Ultimately, AI is not here to replace your job, but rather to help you do your job better (What's Behind the Resistance to Artificial Intelligence? 2018).

Microsoft recently decided to replace dozens of journalists with AI software. These journalists who used to maintain news homepages on MSN website and the Edge browser were informed that robots will be doing their jobs. As part of a global shift away from humans and towards automated updates for news, AI will be selecting, editing, and curating new articles (Microsoft is Replacing its Employees with AI Software, 2020).

According to a report from the World Economic Forum (WEF) called "The Future of Jobs 2018," AI in the workplace is expected to displace 75 million jobs by 2022. However, AI is also expected to create 133 million new roles, providing a net gain of 58 million new jobs in the next few years. These new roles are expected to see a major shift in quality, location, and permanence. As a result, organizations are expected to expand the use of contractors doing specific work and make use of remote staffing. It is critical that organizations play an active role in supporting their existing workforce through reskilling and upskilling, along with individuals taking a proactive approach to their own lifelong learning (Chowdhry, 2018).

SKILLS AND TRAINING

You are not going to need a degree in AI to start applying it to your use cases. Possibly a course or two might be enough. In some cases, reading few pages of some specific example on the web might do the trick to get started. Basic AI techniques to address simple issues may require only the understanding of high-school math and can be accomplished in matter of a day to a week, especially for self-augmentation.

AI JOBS

When seeking the best opportunities for the future, few areas stand out just as much as AI. A Gartner 2019 study showed that enterprise AI applications have risen by 270% in four years, driving a level of demand that exceeds the existing supply of eligible job applicants. This is excellent news for professionals looking in AI. The number of industries using AI is also growing to the point that this rapidly evolving technology transition will leave almost no major enterprise untouched.

The following are the most in-demand AI jobs, with their percentage growth from 2015 to 2019:
- Machine Learning Engineer: 344%
- Robotics Engineer: 128%

- Computer Vision Engineer: 116%
- Data Scientist: 78%

(Johnson, 2020)

CHAPTER 5
ADOPTION

Image by Brigitte Ferauge from Pixabay

AUTOMATION

AI is not just automation, it is better. However, in most cases a digital system and/or automation is a prerequisite. The basic flow is that you take a manual process, automate it, and make the automation intelligent by the application of AI. You can also combine that automation and application of AI in a single implementation.

AI adoption is not a matter of if but rather when. Virtually every process and job can be improved with the application of AI. Not having it, with be a competitive disadvantage. Instead, it needs to be embraced.

CULTURAL RESISTANCE

While clear advantages from AI are becoming increasingly evident, there is resistance to adoption.

Based on a recent survey conducted by O'Reilly, "company culture" was noted to be the major bottleneck for AI adoption in their organizations. Despite the buzz regarding AI, most people in organizations do not yet recognize the need for AI. Executives face three common barriers in every organization – getting started, doubts around functionality and viability, and budget and buy-in (Kesari, 2019).

NEW OFFERINGS

A new product and/or service based on AI can certainly provide a competitive advantage. For example, imagine creating a customer-facing chatbot that can interface with your clients to provide personalize support. Or creating a robot curbside drop off from a restaurant to your car for a food pickup. The possibilities are endless. To get started you need to determine the opportunity, return on investment, etc. and get buy in from the organization to launch the project.

PROCESS IMPROVEMENTS

While there are numerous new product and services opportunities for organizations, you do not need to create new AI products and/or services to start your adoption journey. You can improve what you have existing. This is an easier way to get started.

For example, if you have a process where data is being processed manually form a document and/or database, that is a simple candidate without developing extensive ML techniques. NLP can be utilized to automate the process.

SELF-AUGMENTATION

There have been numerous times in my career when work became monotonous and I was not learning anything new. If no process improvements nor new product and/or services opportunities are available for AI adoption, then you can simply apply AI to your own or your team's tasks and workload. This can bring new level of energy and excitement for yourself. This will be the easiest way to get started on your journey of adopting AI. This can save you time and effort and ultimately contribute of organization's bottom-line improvement. These do not need to initially run on your production servers. They can run on development or test systems with yourself as human backup if something fails.

RISKS

Improving strategic execution with machine learning (2018) further claims, that five years in the future, those who adopted AI early will achieve progress that cannot be copied, nor fast track as with other areas, due to specific ML models and algorithms that are developed and utilized by organizations. Many organizations will need to transform their cultures and operations to some level to take advantage of the AI adoption. However, organizations that do not invest in AL now, along with the necessary changes, risk being left behind.

CHAPTER 6
STRATEGIES

Image by Kiquebg from Pixabay

PIONEERS

Organizations such as IBM, Microsoft, Amazon, Google, Facebook, Tesla, Uber, etc. who have contributed to the AI domain are already benefitting from being in the space. They are in the minority. However, a high majority of organizations still need to adopt and implement AI.

BUILD VERSUS BUY

Virtually every organization is being inundated with AI vendors who claim to improve efficiencies and bottom-line. Vendors are certainly valuable when time-to-market conditions must be met, especially in the competitive AI landscape. I have personally witnessed countless situations where vendors were not only invaluable to my organization's success, but directly to my own success. In addition, some of the most competent and dedicated team members I have worked with were and continue to be vendor employees.

However, without fundamental knowledge in AI, it is risky to engage with vendors for the following reasons.

1. There are numerous different platforms for AI such as IBM Watson, Amazon Lex, Microsoft Azure Machine Learning, Google Kubeflow, TensorFlow, Scikit-Learn, etc. You need to determine which one will best integrate and/or be interoperable with your organization's technology ecosystem. Establishing your own desired platform(s) with some initial internal work will simplify your vendor selection process with regards to platform.

2. AI systems continue to evolve. For example, if you are developing a ML system, you will need to continuously evolve your models as your data increases in size. Initially when you have small set of data, a simple ML model might be sufficient for your needs. However, as the data increases in volume, you will need to update or tune your models or move to ANNs or to deep learning models. If this is not done, you will experience over-fitting condition, where you have more data than needed by the model. And in the unlikely case where the data may decrease, you experience under-fitting. The point being made here is the data will most likely increase and models must adapt. As a result, unless you develop internal competency in AI, your reliance on vendors will be permanent. AI is here to stay.

3. Vendor solutions do not provide competitive advantage. If vendors can make for you, they can do the same for your competitors.

In summary, vendors can be critical to our success when they are utilized as strategic partners, with internal competency to collaborate with them and evaluate their output.

A low-risk, simple, and achievable implementation strategy starts with self-augmentation, then moves to process improvements, and ends up at AI or AI-enabled new projects and/or services.

Adoption Journey	Pros	Cons
Self-Augmentation	Easiest to implement. ROI not needed to get started. Establishes basic AI competency and platform. Low risk as it impacts only oneself.	Improvement only to own productivity.
Process Improvement	Easier to implement. Can be achieved by same technical team with basic AI training. Establishes standardized AI competency and platform.	Minor risk as correlation to before and after needs to be made and only acceptable results will establish adoption.

New Products/Services	Will expand and enhance products and/or services. Create new opportunities and revenue stream(s) for the organization. Establishes mature AI competency and platform.	Risky as this will be trending new space and uncertainty. Only acceptable risk level will establish adoption.

Organizations should consider this path to build their internal competency with self-augmentation, which can be potentially used for process improvement. Once process improvement is done internally, then development of new products and services can be a viable option, along with potential strategic vendor engagements.

CENTER OF EXCELLENCE

The disruptions that will be delivered through AI adoption will require a system in place to execute. This system of people, processes, resources, etc. will be the Center of Excellence (COE).

Also known as competency or capability center, a COE provides shared facilities and resources. As organizations are becoming more complex, teams are often working in silos and not sharing their knowledge, regardless of the concurrent development of different competencies. COEs define these areas and pool internal resources so that they can be shared between groups. This not only brings more efficiencies in an organization, but also creates more consistent experience across the organization. And since COEs are designed to drive innovation and enhancement, they also create an organizational structure that encourages the various members to measure, experiment, and push each other forward (Hou, n.d.).

RETOOLING

While cost-effective AI platform and APIs are available from vendors such as IBM, Amazon, Microsoft, Google, etc., including some with free-tier, going the open-source route might be a good option to get started. In addition to being free of cost, open-source installation offers on-premises options.

- **Open-Source:** Google Kubeflow, TensorFlow, Scikit-Learn, OpenAI, etc.
- **Programming Languages:** Any would be fine. However, Python and R have lots of support for AI.

INNOVATION CENTER

Everyone has bright ideas and talent. Organizations need to be inclusive of everyone in when seeking the spark of creativity and innovation. A simple web form to collect and rate ideas will invite the culture of collective ownership of meaningful transformations.

AI TOOLS TO IMPROVE EFFICIENCY

Poolwan & Smanchat (2018) claim while ML has been adopted by organizations to utilize data for their strategic decision making, it requires technical skills to realize this capability. Despite the availability of software libraries to simplify the development of ML systems from vendors like Amazon and Tensor Flow, data preprocessing, selecting appropriate ML models, and hyperparameter tuning, etc., are challenging tasks that are necessary before it fed to ML systems. This adoption of ML can be a barrier for small organizations with limited resources and knowledge of the domain.

As the demand for ML has been rising over the past years, so has the need for skilled data scientists and other related professionals to make it possible. This has posed a challenge for many organizations with regards to skilled workforce and its associated costs.

AutoML offers relief enabling non-experts to engage effectively in the ML workflow. AutoML tends to automate the maximum number of steps in an ML pipeline, with a minimum effort from humans, without compromising the model's performance. This will assist organizations with their efficiency. Japan's popular shopping app, Mercari, has been using AutoML Vision (Google's AutoML implementation) for the classification of images. While with their own TensorFlow model Mercari achieved 75% accuracy, their transition to AutoML delivered 91.3%, increasing their accuracy by more than 15% (Pandey, 2019).

IBM's AutoAI also simplifies the efforts of the data scientist. It is a new tool that automates numerous complex and time-consuming tasks, without the need for expertise in data science. AutoAI beat 90% of the participating data scientists, in a recent competition for predicting consumer credit risk. AutoAI runs estimators against small subsets of the data to pick the best model effectively. In this iterative process, the sample of the data is progressively through – eliminating estimators. This approach ensures the best estimator is chosen while saving time and storage of the computation. As a result, what could take days or weeks to accomplish, now only takes minutes (Castañón, 2019).

HACKATHONS

There are some environments that create a level of energy, drive, and fun that is conducive to creativity, innovation, productivity, etc. Hackathon is one of them. Enter a hackathon zone is like entering a party where we are going to have fun while undertaking challenges.

Hackathons are generally used to refer to short innovation events where enthusiastic entrepreneurs and software developers spend a day or two in a confined space and challenge them to create some cool application. The same principles are also employed by businesses to break through organizational inertia and to instill more innovation in their cultures. Hackathons can be modified to greatly accelerate the process of digital transformation. By giving management and others the ability to experience collaborative design practices, 24-hour hackathons can demonstrate that large organizations can deliver breakthrough innovation at startup speed (Grijpink, Lau, & Vara, 2015).

However, hackathons are not only designed to solve the problems. They are becoming very impactful ways for organizations to find skilled recruiting workers, come up with new product concepts or use cases, and even train current employees on new business procedures. These events have clear benefits over traditional processes of innovation and problem solving (How to Organize a Hackathon in 6 Simple Steps, n.d.).

I have experienced many hackathons in my career. There were cases where we delivered a week's worth of work in a 24-hour or less continuous shift, with food, caffeine, games, etc. Among other things, a hackathon can provide a very supportive, motivating, and engaging environment where the impossible will seem possible.

I have hosted some hackathons where we learned and delivered a proof-of-concept in area unfamiliar to us in two days. We would learn the concepts on the first day and develop a functional prototype the next day. With regard to adopting AI in an organization, a hackathon with the learning component would spark interest, excitement, and accomplishment. Imagine what going from no competency in AI to having a group of individuals not only gaining fundamental knowledge but also developing a functional application would do their confidence level in a matter of two to three days? It would do wonders!

TEAM INNOVATION DAYS

Team innovation days is a concept that I found opportunities in my career to implement and had success with. When our organizations were not able to provide time for innovation, we found a way to do it ourselves. Let us take an example of a team of four engineers who are not finding the time to innovate in their day jobs. They establish that on Fridays, three of them will do innovative work, where the remaining one will do the day job of the entire team on a rotational basis. As a result, everyone in the team will have an innovation day for three out of four weeks. The breakdown of how many will be participating in the innovation day can vary on team size, what type of work they are doing, and during different phases of their work or projects. However, this concept provides a systematic manner in doing innovative work within a team. This example was for engineers but can be leveraged for many other types of teams as well.

All these concepts discussed above provide a foundation for doing AI work.

CHAPTER 7
PROJECT

Image by Ronald Carreño from Pixabay

FICTITIOUS COMPANY

While we discussed the concepts of AI and the need for embracement and adoption, it is important to see an implementation to drive the message home. We will present a relatively common situation facing many organizations today, with a fictitious company, Alpha Corp, and team.

PROBLEM STATEMENT

Alpha Corp has been performing mediocre due to it high-turnover rate. After some analysis, it was determined that after losing some critical clients, budgets were cuts across the board, including in the technology group. As a result, the software development teams did not receive the funding to upgrade their old technology platform, tools, etc. With no new projects in the pipeline and only support work for their existing installation base, these teams were essentially doing monotonous work, adversely affecting their creative side.

OPPORTUNITY

Alpha Corp has an application, CancerRisk, that needs some updates. Based on the following symptoms or features collected and processed from user surveys, the application predicts if someone is as risk of getting the cancer disease.

- Pain: Bone cancer often hurts from the beginning. Some brain tumors cause headaches that last for days and do not get better with treatment. Pain can also be a late sign of cancer.

- Weight loss without trying. Almost half of people who have cancer lose weight. It is often one of the signs that they notice first.
- Fatigue. If you are tired all the time and rest does not help. Leukemia often wears you out, or you could have blood loss from colon or stomach cancer. Cancer-related weight loss can leave you exhausted, too.
- Fever. If it is high or lasts more than 3 days. Some blood cancers, like lymphoma, cause a fever for days or even weeks.
- Changes in your skin. You may have unusual or new moles, bumps, or marks on your body which could be sign of skin cancer. Your skin can also provide clues to other kinds of cancers. If it is darkened, looks yellow or red, itches, or sprouts more hair, or if you have an unexplained rash, it could be a sign of liver, ovarian, or kidney cancer or lymphoma.
- Sores that do not heal. Spots that bleed and would not go away are also signs of skin cancer. Oral cancer can start as sores in your mouth. If you smoke, chew tobacco, or drink a lot of alcohol, you are at higher risk (Common Signs and Symptoms of Cancer, n.d.).

The following figure illustrates the flow of the system. User inputs are entered into CancerRisk which is a rules-based system that is hard-coded with logic to process them to generate an appropriate result.

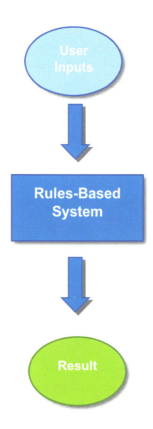

A request has been made to update the CancerRisk to add the following features as well into its logic.

- Cough or hoarseness that does not go away. A cough is one sign of lung cancer, and hoarseness may mean cancer of your voice box (larynx) or thyroid gland.
- Unusual bleeding. Cancer can make blood show up where it should not be. Blood in your feces is a symptom of colon or rectal cancer. And tumors along your urinary tract can cause blood in your urine.
- Anemia. This is when your body does not have enough red blood cells, which are made in your bone marrow. Cancers like leukemia, lymphoma, and multiple myeloma can damage your marrow. Tumors that spread there from other places might crowd out regular red blood cells (Common Signs and Symptoms of Cancer, n.d.).

The typical high-level process that would need to be followed to fulfill this request would be to do the following.
- Business Analysis: Analyze the requirements.
- Software Development: Update the existing software to accommodate the two new parameters.
- Testing: Test the software.
- Deployment: Deploy the software to production.

This was an opportunity for Team Beta to upgrade CancerRisk to become AI-enabled. With AI, less updates to the code base would be needed in the future, reducing the need for system rework.

The following figure illustrates the flow of the proposed system. User inputs will be fed into an AI model that can be trained by data to process the inputs to generate an appropriate result.

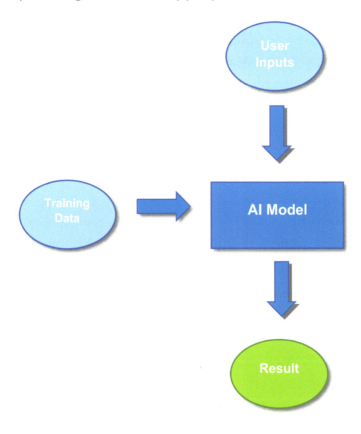

The distinguishing factor for the AI model-based system is that it will not need to be updated for logic changes resulting in less frequent updates. Logic changes can be accomplished by feeding the system with training data. Reusing the system in such scaling scenarios, will reduce risk, save costs, etc.

The most effective way to improve productivity for the SDLC is to reuse code.

The team analyzed the scope of this upgrade and determined that it needed 40-hours of time, which also included learning, and no material cost using open-source framework, i.e., Python programming language and its libraries.

After discussing with their manager, they were not able to secure funding for any additional time needed to make this upgrade possible.

IMPLEMENTATION

Although initially disappointed, the team was determined to make this happen. They devised a scheme where they will break up the development in five 8-hour slots. This way, every member of the team will have one part to develop. This will be completed in five days, where one-member will work on the upgrade development and the other four working on their normal "day-job" and filling the gap of the one missing to do the development. This planned appeared reasonable to the team's manager and provided the approval to start the work.

Team Beta was successful in achieving their goal of upgrading CancerRisk to CancerRisk Pro to be enabled with AI. They performed a demo for their stakeholders. The following table illustrates the application execution.

Data Set (labels with numeric magnitude of scale, with result in the last column):

Pain	Weight Loss	Fatigue	Fever	Skin Changes	Sores	Cough	Bleeding	Anemia	Result
10	10	10	10	10	10	10	10	10	1
1	1	1	1	1	1	1	1	1	0
5	5	5	5	5	5	5	5	5	0
4	4	4	4	4	4	4	4	4	0
1	2	3	4	5	4	2	2	2	0
9	9	8	10	7	8	8	8	8	1
6	7	7	10	10	7	9	9	9	1
3	2	2	1	2	5	2	2	2	0
2	4	8	7	7	1	2	2	2	0
5	8	2	8	4	7	7	7	7	1

This dataset was created based on the fundamental principle that as the magnitude of each feature increases, so does being at risk for cancer. The values in the data set were established with the following set of logic.
- Value of 10 would be of the highest magnitude.

- Value of 1 would be of the lowest magnitude.
- Each feature will have a value between 1 – 10, based on the level of a symptom being experienced.
- The result of each record or row will be either 1 or 0, for being at risk for cancer or not, respectively.
- The first record has magnitude of 10 for all the features and results in a 1 for clearly being at risk of cancer.
- The second record has magnitude of 1 for all the features and results in a 0 for clearly not being at risk for cancer.
- Other eight-records have varying range of magnitudes and results.

The following is the actual output from the program execution/run:

```
==========
Enter the training dataset file name: cancer-
detection.csv

Enter a value from 1 to 10, for each feature,
with 10 being of highest magnitude.
Pain : 1
Weight Loss  : 2
Fatigue : 2
Fever : 1
Skin Changes  : 2
Sores  : 3
Cough  : 1
```

```
Bleeding : 3
Anemia : 1
* * * * * * * * * * * * * * * * * * * * * * * * * * * * * * * * * * * * * * *
[1 2 2 1 2 3 1 3 1]
[[1 2 2 1 2 3 1 3 1]]
Probability:  [[0.84268857 0.15731143]]
Prediction:  [0]
Your likelihood for this is negative.
* * * * * * * * * * * * * * * *********************

==========
```

In real cases, you will need more than 10 data points in order to have a model that can be relied upon.

During the demo, Jim, a member of the HR team walks by and noticed the excitement from the team. He joins the meeting to see what this was all about. He was astonished to learn that Team Beta developed a system that can be trained to determine who is as risk of cancer purely from the training data fed into the system. He immediately pondered about a situation about several potential candidates who are nearing final stage of the interview process that are pending an assessment on their emotional intelligence (EI). He asked the team if he can use this system to train it to predict which candidates will have a high EI. At first the team paused to think whether that would be possible. However, then they concluded that not only it can be trained to predict EI, but just about anything. They cautiously asked Jim to send them the features that would constitute EI and data to train the AI system.

The next day, Jim establishes the following 13 features for an EI user survey.

- Ponder Feelings: This is where self and social awareness is achieved enabling the ability to recognize emotions in both ourselves and others. For example, you can ponder about your emotional strengths and weaknesses.
- Pause: Taking a pause for a moment provides us the opportunity stop and think before we speak or act. This can potentially avoid awkward moments or make premature commitments.
- Control Thoughts: You avoid being a slave to your emotions by trying to control your feelings, allowing yourself to live in a way that is in accordance with your goals and values.
- Welcome Criticism: You keep your feelings in check when you receive negative feedback, and ask yourself: How does this improve me?
- Show Authenticity: You are being authentic when you say what you mean, meaning what you say, and keeping your values and principles above all else.

- Demonstrate Empathy: Being emphatic means that you understand others' thoughts and feelings, which in turn helps you connect with others better.
- Praise Others: All human beings yearn for recognition and appreciation. When you praise others, you will fulfill the desire and develop trust in the process.
- Provide Helpful Feedback: Negative feedback has huge potential to hurt other people's feelings. You reframe criticism as constructive feedback, so the recipient sees it as helpful rather than harmful.
- Apologize: It takes courage and strength to be able to say you are sorry. But doing so displays modesty, a quality that naturally would attract people to you.
- Forgive and Forget: You are preventing others from holding your emotions hostage when you forgive and forget – allowing you to move on.
- Keeping Commitments: When you become accustomed to keeping your word, in big and small things, you develop a strong reputation for reliability and trustworthiness.
- Help Others: One of the best ways of making a positive effect on others' feelings is by helping them.

- Guard Emotions: EI also has a dark side. There are people who try to manipulate the emotions of others to promote a personal agenda or for some other selfish cause. Hence, you need to improve your own EI to protect yourself when they do (Bariso, 2018).

Jim prepares the following dataset based on the established features.

Ponder Feelings	Pause	Control Thoughts	Welcome Criticism	Show Authenticity	Demonstrate Empathy	Praise Others	Provide Helpful Feedback	Apologize	Forgive and Forget	Keep Commitments	Help Others	Guard Emotions	Result
10	10	10	10	10	10	10	10	10	10	10	10	10	1
1	1	1	1	1	1			1	1	1	1	1	0
5	5	5	5	5	5	5	5	5	5	5	5	5	0
4	4	4	4	4	4	4	4	4	4	4	4	4	0
5	4	3	4	5	4	2	2	2	4	5	4	2	0
7	8	8	10	7	8	8	8	8	10	7	8	8	1
10	7	7	1	10	7	9	9	9	1	10	7	9	1
7	5	2	7	2	5	2	2	2	7	2	5	1	0
2	1	8	8	7	1	2	2	2	8	7	1	2	0
4	7	2	8	4	7	7	7	7	8	4	7	7	1

This dataset was created based on the similar fundamental principle as for detecting cancer use case. As the magnitude of each feature increases, so does the possibility of being emotionally intelligent. The values in the data set were established with the following set of logic.

- Value of 10 would be of the highest magnitude.
- Value of 1 would be of the lowest magnitude.
- Each feature will have a value between 1 – 10, based on the level of an indicator being experienced.
- The result of each record or row will be either 1 or 0, for being emotionally intelligent or not, respectively.
- The first record has magnitude of 10 for all the features and results in a 1 for clearly being emotionally intelligent.
- The second record has magnitude of 1 for all the features and results in a 0 for clearly not being emotionally intelligent.
- Other eight-records have varying range of magnitudes and results.

The team runs the application against the EI data set to see for themselves before presenting to Jim. And then the magic happens! It works! They renamed the application from CancerRisk Pro to

General-Purpose Prediction System (GPPS). The scope of possibilities for Team Beta's GPPS just increased tremendously. They conducted a demo for Jim and the entire HR team.

The following is the actual output from the program execution/run:

```
==========
Enter the training dataset file name:
emotional-intelligence.csv

Enter a value from 1 to 10, for each feature,
with 10 being of highest magnitude.
Feelings Awareness : 10

Pause : 8

Control Thoughts : 7

Welcome Criticism : 7


...

Your likelihood for this is positive.
*************************************

==========
```

The above output is limited. It only displays the beginning and the end. Note that the file name has changed, since the execution of the CancerRisk program, and the fields established for EI are being displayed and processed.

The following is the source code in the Python language for the GPPS:

```
==========
## Import Appropriate Libraries
# Data Analysis
import pandas as pd
# Scientific Computing
import numpy as np
# ML Model
from sklearn.linear_model import
LogisticRegression
# Creating/Loading Model
import pickle

print("*************************************")
print("* General Purpose Prediction System *")
print("*************************************\n"
)

## Load Data
dataset_file = input ("Enter the training
dataset file name: ")
df = pd.read_csv(dataset_file)

## Convert to Array
trainingResult = np.array(df["Result"])
trainingData = np.array(df.drop("Result",
axis=1))

## Create ML Model
pickledModel =
pickle.dumps(LogisticRegression().fit(trainingD
ata, trainingResult))

## Load ML Model
loadedModel = pickle.loads(pickledModel)

## Collect Data from User
i=0
input_array = []
length = len(df.columns)
```

```
print("\nEnter a value from 1 to 10, for each
feature, with 10 being of highest magnitude.")

for i in range(length-1):
    input_array.append(int(input(df.columns[i]
+ " : ")))

print("************************************")
featureVaribles = np.array(input_array)
print(featureVaribles)
featureVaribles = np.reshape(featureVaribles,
(1,length-1))
print(featureVaribles)

# Make Prediction
resultPrediction =
loadedModel.predict(featureVaribles)
resultPredictionProbability =
loadedModel.predict_proba(featureVaribles)
print("Probability: ",
resultPredictionProbability)
print("Prediction: ", resultPrediction)
if(resultPrediction==1):
    print("Your likelihood for this is
positive.")
else:
    print("Your likelihood for this is
negative.")
print("************************************")
========
```

Although the situation, organization, and team are fictitious, the GPPS is real, including the application executions depicted in the two runs above. This system takes a dataset file in comma-separate-values (CSV) format, trains a ML Logistic Regression model, and processes the inputs against the model to generate an appropriate result.

In reality, this solution should include model testing and validation of AI model so that it will good enough to be used. In addition, it should not take 40-hours to develop. This number was chosen for our fictitious example for the simplicity of math. A developer with AI experience can easily do this in a few hours. One without AI experience may take possibly one more day.

The primary reason to include source code, less than 60 lines of code including comments, is to demonstrate the simplicity by which we can adapt AI to our technology eco system. In addition, it is important to witness that one code base can solved problems in multiple domains with merely different data sets used for training. Just like humans can be trained to do different things, so can machines.

The example was for a situation where execution was done without any financial support. The two sets of source code for the automation and AI system that were provided were very simplistic. That was done primarily for the purpose of distinguishing between automation and AI. In addition, it was to demonstrate AI's scalability in solving different problems using same system with different dataset.

CHAPTER 8
FUTURE OF AI, SUMMARY, AND CONCLUSION

Image by Tumisu from Pixabay

READING THOUGHTS

In 2018, MIT Media Lab unveiled the project AlterEgo, a prototype that can "read" your mind. It is a non-invasive, wearable, peripheral neural interface that enables humans to converse in natural language with machines, AI assistants, services, and other people simply by articulating words internally. This is achieved without any voice, opening their mouth, and/or externally observable movements. The user feedback is given through audio, and through bone conduction, without disturbing the usual auditory perception of the user, and making the interface closed loop. It creates an interaction between person and machine that is subjectively perceived as being totally internal to the human user – like as speaking to one's self (Project AlterEgo, n.d.).

A primary goal of this project is to better interact with people with speech disabilities in conditions such as ALS and MS. In addition, the program has the ability to easily combine people and computers. This includes computing, the Internet, and AI can weave into our everyday lives as a "second self" and improve our knowledge and abilities (Project AlterEgo, n.d.).

HARDWARE ADVANCEMENT

MIT's miniature new artificial brain chip advances the possibility of delivering supercomputer level smarts to mobile devices. MIT researchers have published a paper that describes a new type of artificial brain synapse offering amazing performance improvements which can be combined in quantities of tens of thousands on a chip smaller than a single piece of confetti. As a result, it can enable complex AI computations locally on devices, while being small and power-efficient, and without needing to establish connectivity to data centers (Etherington, 2020).

Summary

AI is a vast and complex domain which can take years to master with the combination of appropriate training and application. However, there is enough supporting material to get started in your journey. This involves systematically starting out with smaller scope tasks and undertaking more and more complex ones. Consider AI your partner in success, which frees you from mundane tasks to focus on creativity and innovation.

Unlike humans, where it can take years to learn or master something, AI can learn almost immediately and enter in our domains and space. By today's standards, the adoption of AI is becoming a necessity for survival rather than a distinguishing factor. Just like it is unimaginable not using computers, we need to start thinking similarly about AI. And think of AI as advanced IT, not as a separate thing.

CONCLUSION

AI is unstoppable. It is not stopping for us. We need to get onboard or we will become irrelevant. Hence, we need to think what we will not apply AI to, instead of what to apply too. Choose AI today so that it can choose you in the future. Be relevant.

REFERENCES

Adapt and thrive. (2019). *MIT Sloan Management Review, 60*(3), 1-23. Retrieved from https://search.proquest.com/docview/2227 406242?accountid=158798

Ali, F. (2018, March 31). Culinary Artificial Intelligence. Retrieved May 15, 2020, from https://medium.com/@faris.ali/culinary-artificial-intelligence-11a2a8dc05f7

Amrit, P. S., & Singh, G. (2019). Analysis of amazon product reviews using big data-apache pig tool. *International Journal of Information Engineering and Electronic Business, 11*(1), 11. doi:http://dx.doi.org/10.5815

Artificial Superintelligence (ASI). (n.d.). Retrieved November 03, 2020, from https://www.techopedia.com/definition/31 619/artificial-superintelligence-asi

Assem, H., Xu, L., Buda, T. S., & O'sullivan, D. (2016). Machine learning as a service for enabling internet of things and people. *Personal and Ubiquitous*

Computing, 20(6), 899-914.
doi:http://dx.doi.org/10.1007/s00779-016-
0963-3

Bariso, J. (2018, February 28). 13 Signs of High
Emotional Intelligence. Retrieved
August 22, 2020, from
https://www.inc.com/justin-bariso/13-
things-emotionally-intelligent-people-
do.html

Castañón, J. (2019, October 15). AutoAI: The
Secret Sauce. Retrieved November 21,
2020, from
https://towardsdatascience.com/autoai-
the-secret-sauce-f42e80b90070

Chowdhry, A. (2018, September 18). Artificial
Intelligence to Create 58 Million New
Jobs by 2022, Says Report. Retrieved
October 08, 2020, from
https://www.forbes.com/sites/amitchowdh
ry/2018/09/18/artificial-intelligence-to-
create-58-million-new-jobs-by-2022-says-
report

Common Signs and Symptoms of Cancer. (n.d.).
Retrieved August 21, 2020, from

https://www.webmd.com/cancer/understanding-cancer-symptoms

D Asir Antony, G. S., Leavline, E. J., Muthukrishnan, S., & Yuvaraj, R. (2018). Machine learning based business forecasting. *International Journal of Information Engineering and Electronic Business, 10*(6), 40. doi:http://dx.doi.org/10.5815/ijieeb.2018.06.05

Dean, S. (2020, February 27). The new burger chef makes $3 an hour and never goes home. (It's a robot). Retrieved March 14, 2020, from https://www.latimes.com/business/technology/story/2020-02-27/flippy-fast-food-restaurant-robot-arm

Deep Neural Network. (n.d.). Retrieved November 18, 2020, from https://www.techopedia.com/definition/32902/deep-neural-network

Dimitrovska, I., & Malinovski, T. (2017). Creating a business value while transforming data assets using machine learning. *Computer Engineering and*

Applications Journal, 6(2), 59-69. Retrieved
from
https://search.proquest.com/docview/2068
426324?accountid=158798

Dormehl, L. (2019, January 06). What is an
artificial neural network? Here's
everything you need to know. Retrieved
February 24, 2020, from
https://www.digitaltrends.com/cool-
tech/what-is-an-artificial-neural-network

Elgammal, A. (n.d.). AI is Blurring the Definition
of Artist. Retrieved November 18,
2020, from
https://www.techopedia.com/definition/32
902/deep-neural-network

Etherington, D. (2020, June 08). MIT's tiny
artificial brain chip could bring
supercomputer smarts to mobile devices.
Retrieved October 21, 2020, from
https://techcrunch.com/2020/06/08/mits-
tiny-artificial-brain-chip-could-bring-
supercomputer-smarts-to-mobile-devices

Ganapathy, K., Abdul, S., & Nursetyo, A. (2018).
Artificial intelligence in

neurosciences: A clinician's perspective. *Neurology India,* 66(4), 934-939. doi:http://dx.doi.org/10.4103/0028-3886.236971

Grijpink, F., Lau, A., & Vara, J. (2015, October 01). Demystifying the hackathon. Retrieved January 03, 2020, from https://www.mckinsey.com/business-functions/mckinsey-digital/our-insights/demystifying-the-hackathon

Hao, K. (2018, November 17). What is machine learning? Retrieved January 16, 2020, from https://www.technologyreview.com/2018/11/17/103781/what-is-machine-learning-we-drew-you-another-flowchart

Heath, N. (2018, August 22). What is artificial general intelligence? Retrieved December 15, 2020, from https://www.zdnet.com/article/what-is-artificial-general-intelligence

Heaven, W. D. (2020, June 12). Facebook just released a database of 100,000 deepfakes to teach AI how to spot them. Retrieved August 14, 2020, from

https://www.technologyreview.com/2020/
06/12/1003475/facebooks-deepfake-
detection-challenge-neural-network-ai

Hendler, J., & Mulvehill, A. M. (2016). *Social
Machines: The Coming Collision of Artificial
Intelligence, Social Networking, and
Humanity.* New York, NY: Apress.

Hou, Z. (n.d.). What Is a Center of Excellence and
Why Do You Need One?
Retrieved December 27, 2020, from
https://www.convinceandconvert.com/soci
al-media-strategy/what-is-a-center-of-
excellence

How to Organize a Hackathon in 6 Simple Steps.
(n.d.). Retrieved December 28,
2020, from
https://corporate.hackathon.com/article-
how-to-organize-a-hackathon

Improving strategic execution with machine
learning. (2018). *MIT Sloan Management
Review, 60*(1), 2-7. Retrieved from
https://search.proquest.com/docview/2112
537500?accountid=158798

Johnson, R. (2020, May 14). Jobs of the Future:

Starting a Career in Artificial
Intelligence. Retrieved July 21, 2020, from
https://www.bestcolleges.com/blog/future-
proof-industries-artificial-intelligence

Joshi, N. (2019, June 19). 7 Types of Artificial
Intelligence. Retrieved May 13, 2020,
from
https://www.forbes.com/sites/cognitivewo
rld/2019/06/19/7-types-of-artificial-
intelligence

Kesari, G. (2019, August 04). How to Beat
Resistance to AI Projects: 3 Steps.
Retrieved October 28, 2020, from
https://towardsdatascience.com/how-to-
beat-resistance-to-ai-projects-3-steps-
bb191c310c4a

Lewis, T. (2014, December 04). A Brief History of
Artificial Intelligence. Retrieved
August 02, 2020, from
https://www.livescience.com/49007-
history-of-artificial-intelligence.html

Liang, T. (1993). Special section: Research in
integrating learning capabilities into
information systems. *Journal of
Management Information Systems, 9*(4), 5.

Retrieved from https://search-proquest-com.ezp-02.lirn.net/docview/218948499?accountid=158798

Marr, B. (2019, April 08). 7 Amazing Examples of Computer and Machine Vision In Practice. Retrieved December 02, 2020, from https://www.forbes.com/sites/bernardmarr/2019/04/08/7-amazing-examples-of-computer-and-machine-vision-in-practice

Martineau, P. (2019, December 20). Facebook Removes Accounts With AI-Generated Profile Photos. Retrieved January 13, 2020, from https://www.wired.com/story/facebook-removes-accounts-ai-generated-photos

Microsoft is Replacing its Employees with AI Software. (2020, June 02). Retrieved August 19, 2020, from https://www.novinite.com/articles/204744/Microsoft+is+Replacing+its+Employees+With+AI+Software

Mizokami, K. (2020, May 22). The Air Force's AI-Powered 'Skyborg' Drones Could

Fly as Early as 2023. Retrieved November 03, 2020, from https://www.yahoo.com/news/air-forces-ai-powered-skyborg-135000735.html

Nieva, R. (2017, July 31). Facebook puts cork in chatbots that created a secret language. Retrieved December 12, 2020, from https://www.cnet.com/news/what-happens-when-ai-bots-invent-their-own-language

O'Carroll, B. (2017, October 24). What are the 3 types of AI? A guide to narrow, general, and super artificial intelligence. Retrieved July 16, 2020, from https://codebots.com/artificial-intelligence/the-3-types-of-ai-is-the-third-even-possible

Pandey, P. (2019, April 18). AutoML: The Next Wave of Machine Learning. Retrieved November 10, 2020, from https://heartbeat.fritz.ai/automl-the-next-wave-of-machine-learning-5494baac615f

Pathak, N. (2017). *Artificial Intelligence for .NET: Speech, Language, and Search*. New York, NY: Apress.

Performance anxiety. (2018, July 05). Retrieved September 20, 2020, from https://www.economist.com/the-world-if/2018/07/05/performance-anxiety

Poolwan, J., & Smanchat, S. (2018). An architecture for simplified and automated machine learning. *International Journal of Electrical and Computer Engineering, 8*(5), 2994-3002. Retrieved from https://search.proquest.com/docview/2124487786?accountid=158798

Porter, J. (2019, April 26). OpenAI's MuseNet generates AI music at the push of a button. Retrieved January 21, 2020, from https://www.theverge.com/2019/4/26/18517803/openai-musenet-artificial-intelligence-ai-music-generation-lady-gaga-harry-potter-mozart

Project AlterEgo. (n.d.). Retrieved August 24, 2020, from https://www.media.mit.edu/projects/alterego/overview

Russell, S., Dewey, D., & Tegmark, M. (2015). Research priorities for robust and beneficial artificial intelligence. *AI Magazine, 36*(4), 105-114. doi:http://dx.doi.org/10.1609/aimag.v36i4. 2577

Sample, I. (2020, January 13). What are deepfakes – and how can you spot them? Retrieved March 14, 2020, from https://www.theguardian.com/technology/ 2020/jan/13/what-are-deepfakes-and-how-can-you-spot-them

Simon, M. (2020, April 16). Everything You Ever Wanted to Know About Robots. Retrieved December 12, 2020, from https://www.wired.com/story/wired-guide-to-robots

Smith, R. G., & Eckroth, J. (2017). Building AI applications: Yesterday, today, and tomorrow. *AI Magazine, 38*(1), 6-22. doi:http://dx.doi.org/10.1609/aimag.v38i1. 2709

Sterne, J. (2017). *Artificial Intelligence for Marketing*. Hoboken, NJ: Wiley.

Stupp, C. (2019, August 30). Fraudsters Used AI to

Mimic CEO's Voice in Unusual Cybercrime Case. Retrieved September 03, 2020, from https://www.wsj.com/articles/fraudsters-use-ai-to-mimic-ceos-voice-in-unusual-cybercrime-case-11567157402

TORRES.AI, J. (2018, September 10). Why now this Artificial Intelligence boom? Retrieved August 16, 2020, from https://towardsdatascience.com/why-now-this-artificial-intelligence-boom-b50a35713090

Watt, J., Borhani, R., & Katsaggelos, A. K. (2016). *Machine Learning Refined*. New York, NY: Cambridge University Press.

What is Robotic Process Automation (RPA)? Everything You Need to Know. (n.d.). Retrieved October 11, 2020, from https://searchcio.techtarget.com/definition/RPA

What's Behind the Resistance to Artificial Intelligence? (2018, August 07). Retrieved September 17, 2020, from https://atimesolutions.com/blog/2018/08/

07/whats-behind-the-resistance-to-artificial-intelligence

Yse, D. L. (2019, January 15). Your Guide to
Natural Language Processing (NLP).
Retrieved October 08, 2020, from
https://towardsdatascience.com/your-
guide-to-natural-language-processing-nlp-
48ea2511f6e1